12/14

Short, Shorter, Shortest

by Rebecca Felix

Ideas for Parents and Teachers

Amicus Readers let children practice reading informational texts at the earliest reading levels. Familiar words and concepts with close photo-text matches support early readers.

Before Reading
- Discuss the cover photo with the child. What does it tell him?
- Ask the child to predict what she will learn in the book.

Read the Book
- "Walk" through the book and look at the photos. Let the child ask questions.
- Read the book to the child, or have the child read independently.

After Reading
- Use the photo quiz at the end of the book to review the text.
- Prompt the child to make connections. Ask: *Can you think of other animals that are short?*

Amicus Readers are published by Amicus P.O. Box 1329, Mankato, MN 56002 www.amicuspublishing.us

Library of Congress Cataloging-in-Publication Data
Felix, Rebecca, 1984-
  Short, shorter, shortest / Rebecca Felix.
    pages cm. -- (Size it up!)
  K to Grade 3.
  Audience: Age 6
ISBN 978-1-60753-575-1 (hardcover) --
ISBN 978-1-60753-613-0 (pdf ebook)
  1. English language--Adjective--Juvenile literature. 2. English language--Comparison--Juvenile literature. I. Title.
  PE1241.F465 2014
  428.2--dc23
                                2013044902

Photo Credits: Eric Isselee/Shutterstock Images, cover (left), cover (middle), 1 (left), 1 (middle), 5 (left), 6-7, 11 (left), 14-15, 16 (top middle), 16 (bottom right); Oksana Kuzmina/Shutterstock Images, cover (bottom right), 1 (bottom right), 5 (right), 16 (top left); Kamenetskiy Konstantin/Shutterstock Images, cover (top right), 1 (top right); Erik Lam/Shutterstock Images, 3; Peter Kirillov/Shutterstock Images, 4, 16 (top right); Tatiana Katsai/Shutterstock Images, 6 (left); Helena Queen/Shutterstock Images, 7 (right); Linn Currie/Shutterstock Images, 8 (left); D and D Photo Sudbury/Shutterstock Images, 8-9; Thinkstock, 9 (right); Shutterstock Images, 10, 11 (right), 13 (left); Sergey Lavrentev/Shutterstock Images, 12; Liliya Kulianionak/Shutterstock Images, 13 (right); Jana Behr/Shutterstock Images, 14 (left), 16 (bottom left); Pavel Hlystov/Shutterstock Images, 15 (right), 16 (bottom middle)

Produced for Amicus by The Peterson Publishing Company and Red Line Editorial.

Editor Jenna Gleisner
Designer Craig Hinton
Printed in the United States of America
Mankato, MN
1-2014
PA10001
10 9 8 7 6 5 4 3 2 1

Dogs measure tall and short. Short means small height or length. How do short dogs compare in size?

beagle

Beagles are short. French bulldogs are shorter. Chihuahuas are the shortest. The shortest is shorter than a can of soup.

French bulldog

Chihuahua

English
bulldog

6

basset
hound

English bulldogs have short legs. Basset hound legs are shorter. Corgi legs are the shortest. Their bodies almost touch the ground.

corgi

Scottish
terrier

Boston
terrier

Scottish terrier tails are short.
Boston terrier tails are shorter.
Mini Australian shepherd tails are
the shortest. Some look like they
do not even have a tail!

mini
Australian
shepherd

German shepherd

German shepherds have short hair. Dalmatian hair is shorter. Greyhound hair is the shortest. Their hair is so short you can almost see their skin!

dalmatian

greyhound

mini
schnauzer

12

malamute

Mini schnauzer ears are short. Malamute ears are shorter. Chow chow ears are the shortest. They can be shorter than the chow chow's hair.

chow chow

boxer

Boxer noses are short. Shih tzu noses are shorter. Pug noses are the shortest. They do not even stick out from their faces!

shih tzu

pug

Which dog is the shortest?
Which dog has the shortest nose?

Chihuahua

French bulldog

beagle

boxer

pug

shih tzu